T0085632

JAKE REICHBART
JAZZ GUITAR CHRISTMAS

2   AWAY IN A MANGER

4   DECK THE HALL

6   THE FIRST NOËL

8   GOD REST YE MERRY, GENTLEMEN

10   HARK! THE HERALD ANGELS SING

12   IT CAME UPON THE MIDNIGHT CLEAR

14   O LITTLE TOWN OF BETHLEHEM

15   SILENT NIGHT

18   WE WISH YOU A MERRY CHRISTMAS

20   WHAT CHILD IS THIS?

23   BIOGRAPHY

To access video visit:
www.halleonard.com/mylibrary

Enter Code
2635-6503-7721-1482

For more information on Jake Reichbart, visit: www.jakereichbart.com

ISBN 978-1-4584-1145-7

HAL•LEONARD®

Visit Hal Leonard Online at
www.halleonard.com

Contact Us:
Hal Leonard
7777 West Bluemound
Road
Milwaukee, WI 53213
Email: info@halleonard.com

In Europe contact:
Hal Leonard Europe Limited
42 Wigmore Street
Marylebone, London, W1U 2RN
Email: info@halleonardeurope.com

In Australia contact:
Hal Leonard Australia Pty. Ltd.
4 Lentara Court
Cheltenham, Victoria, 3192
Australia
Email: info@halleonard.com.au

Away in a Manger

Words John T. McFarland (v.3)
Music by James R. Murray

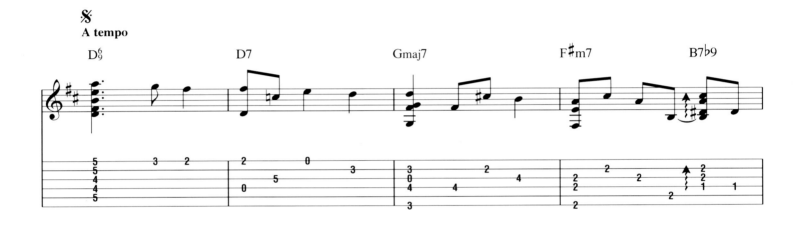

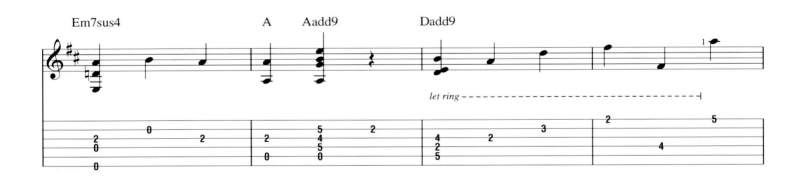

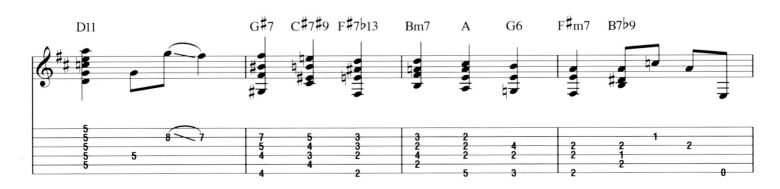

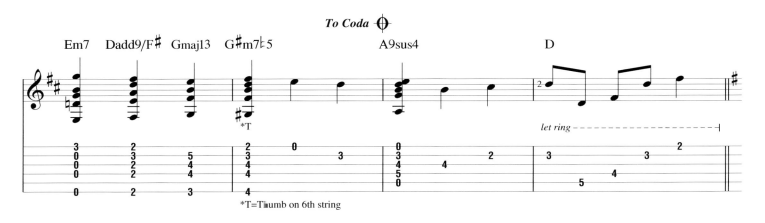

*T=Thumb on 6th string

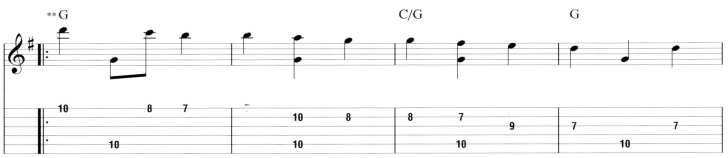

**Chord symbols reflect implied harmony, next 3 meas.

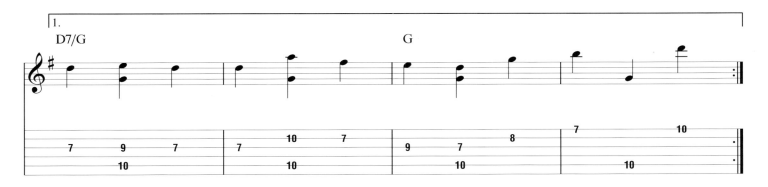

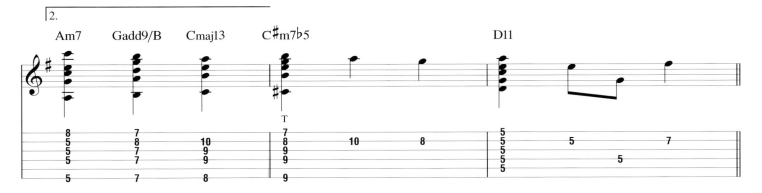

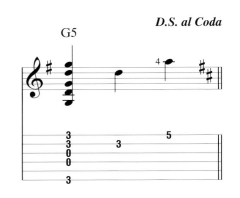

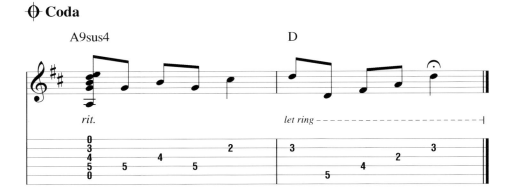

3

Deck the Hall

Traditional Welsh Carol

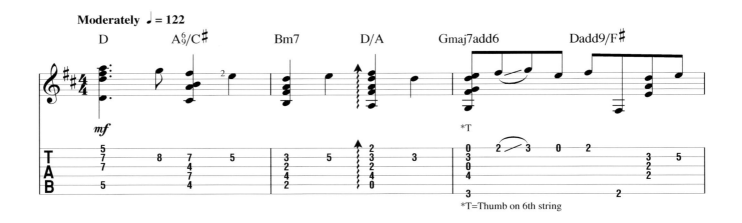

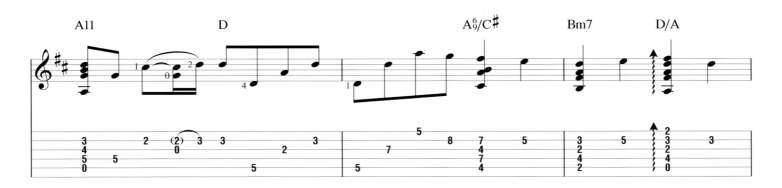

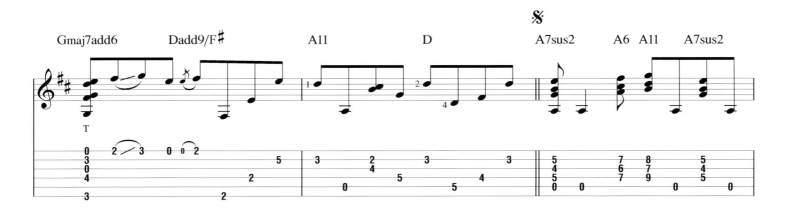

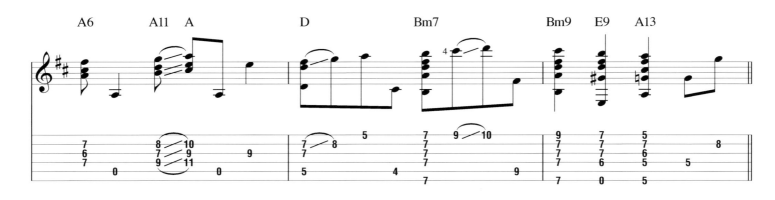

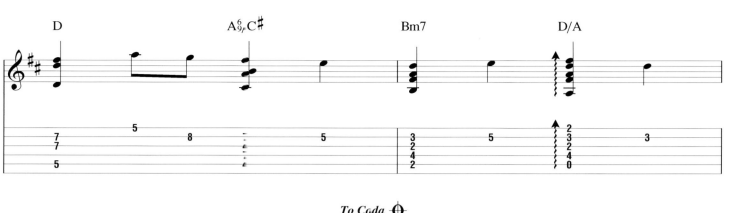

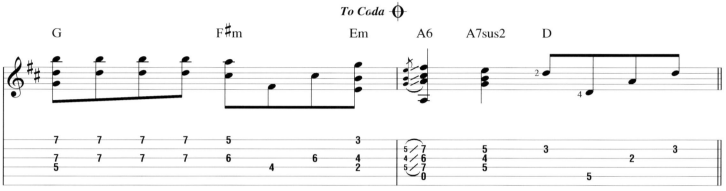

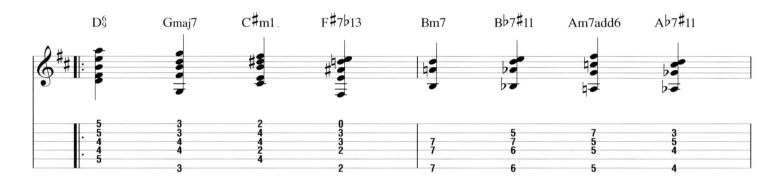

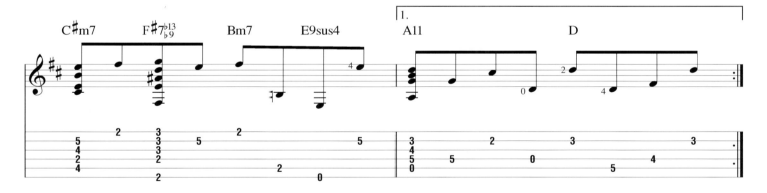

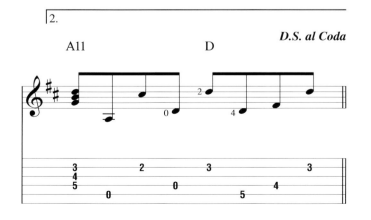

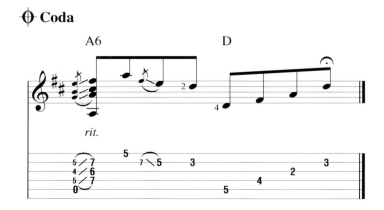

The First Noël

17th Century English Carol
Music from W. Sandys' Christmas Carols

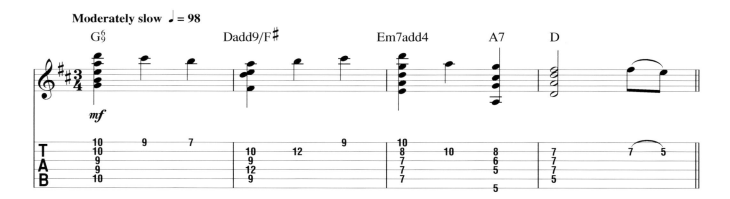

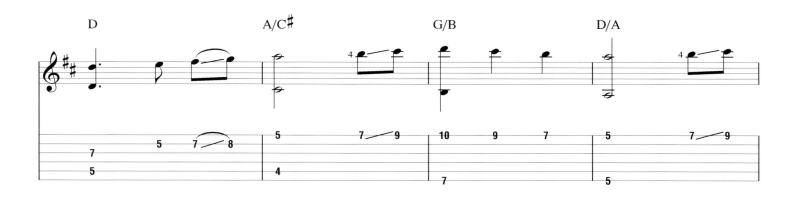

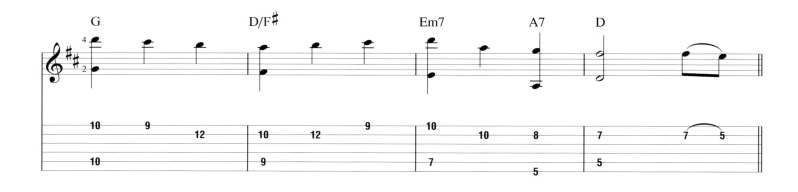

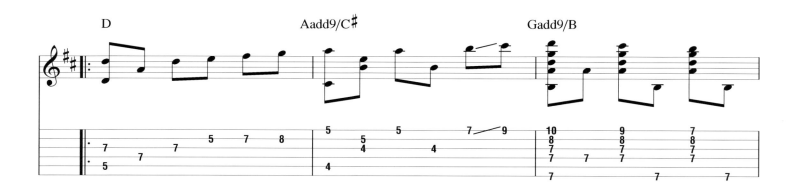

God Rest Ye Merry, Gentlemen

19th Century English Carol

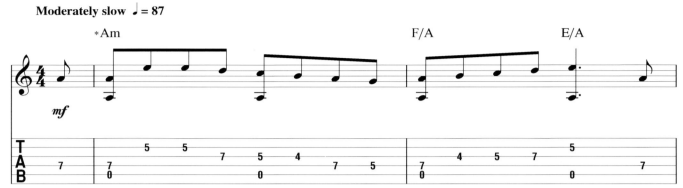

*Chord symbols reflect implied harmony, next 10 meas.

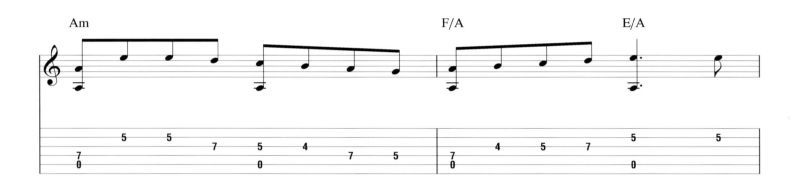

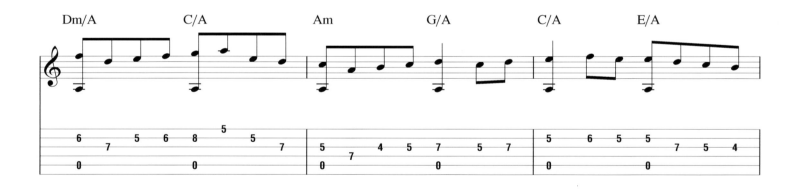

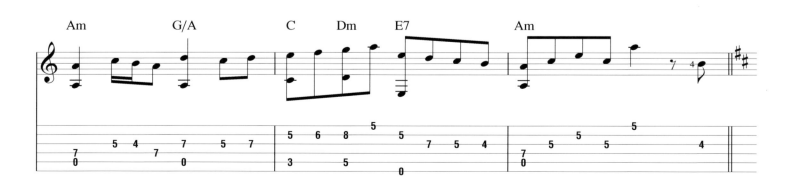

**Optional: Thumb on 6th string

Hark! The Herald Angels Sing

Words Charles Wesley
Altered by George Whitefield
Music by Felix Mendelssohn-Bartholdy

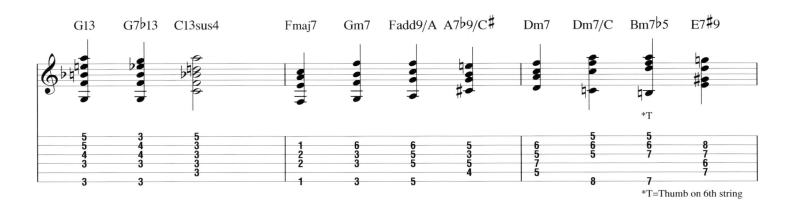

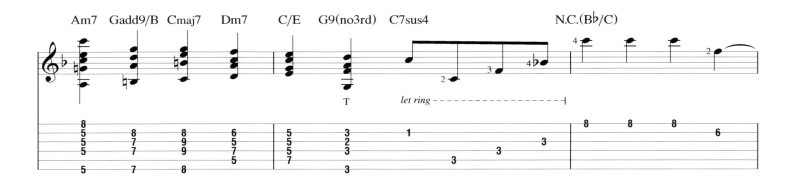

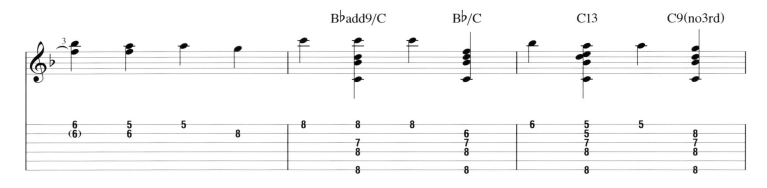

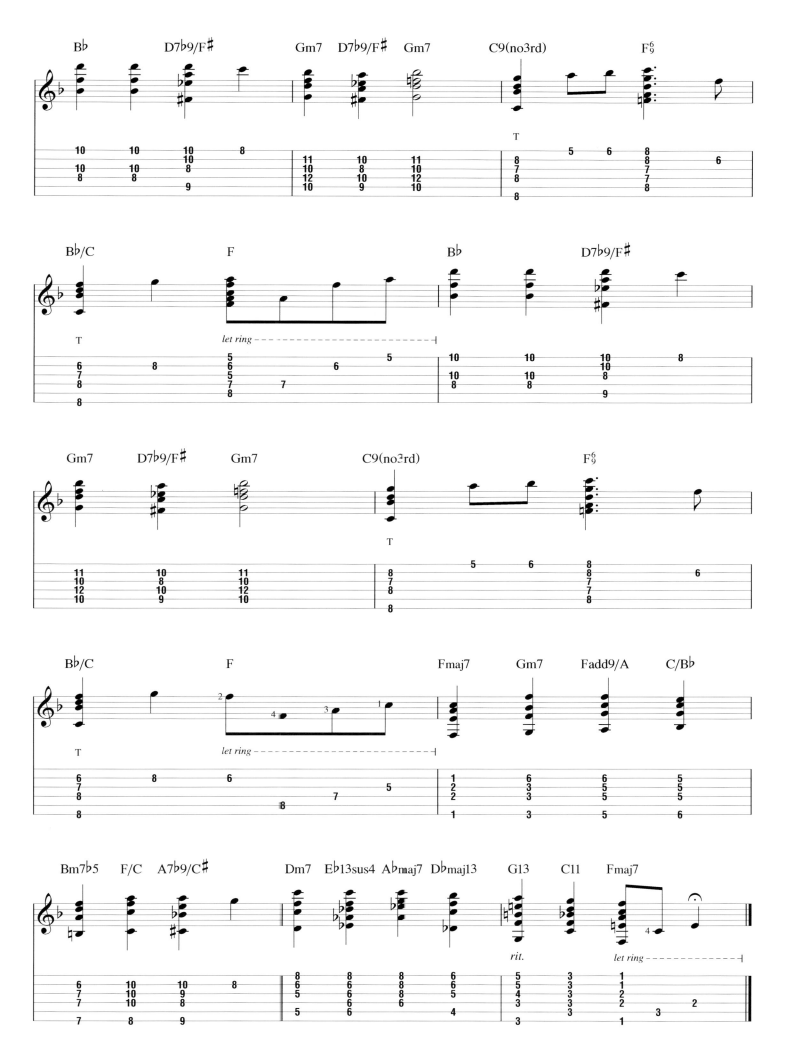

It Came Upon the Midnight Clear

Words by Edmund Hamilton Sears
Music by Richard Storrs Willis

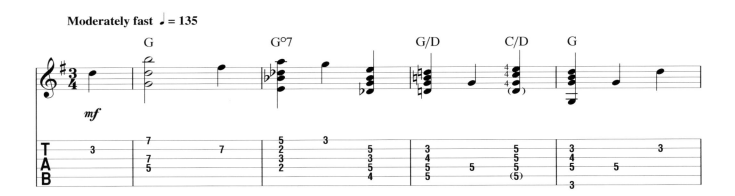

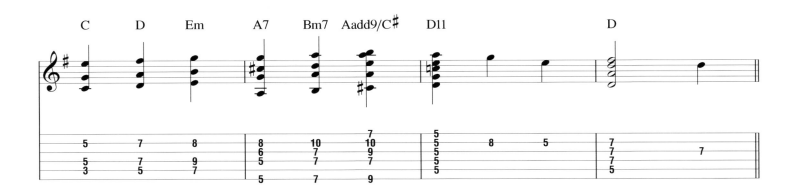

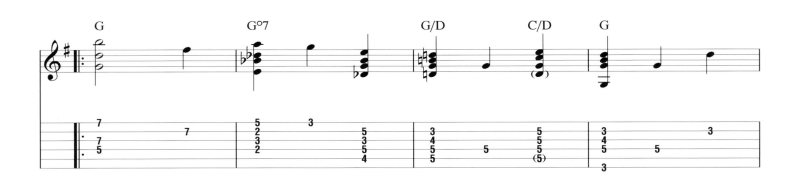

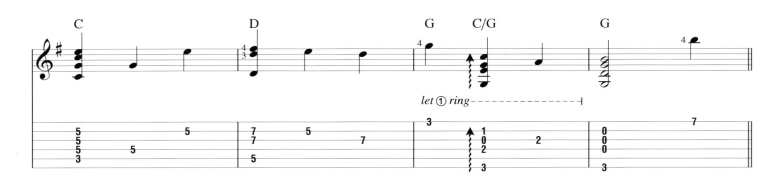

*T=Thumb on 6th string

O Little Town of Bethlehem

Words by Phillips Brooks
Music by Lewis H. Redner

Silent Night

Words by Joseph Mohr
Translated by John F. Young
Music by Franz X. Gruber

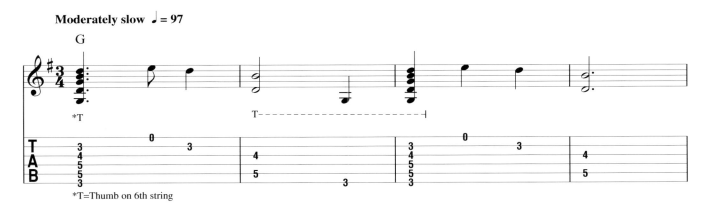

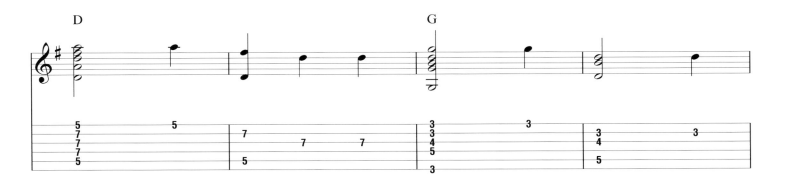

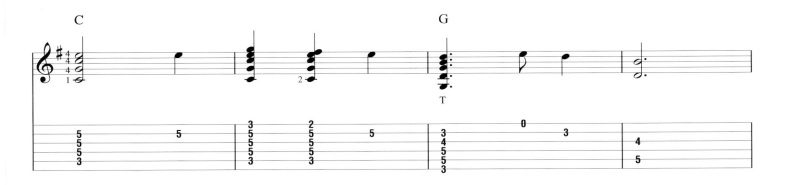

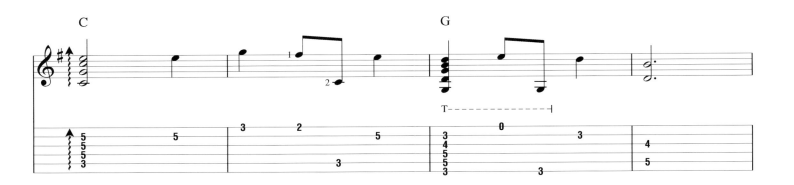

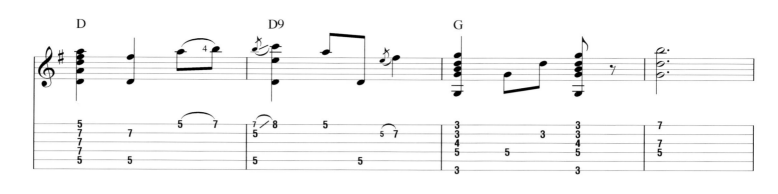

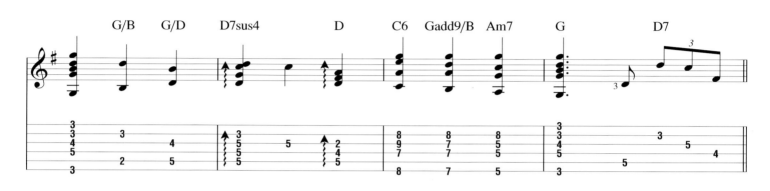

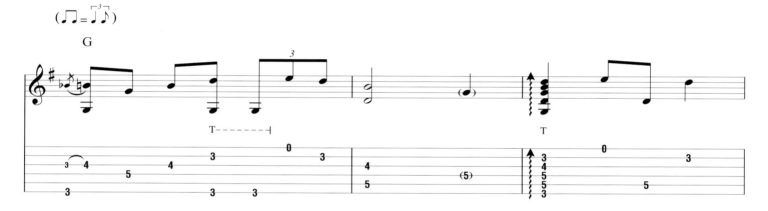

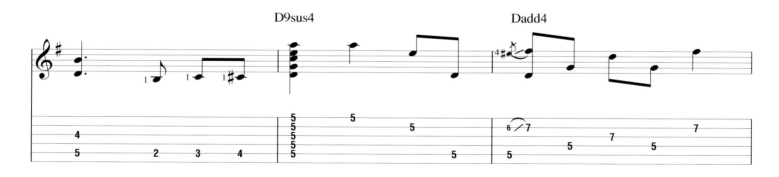

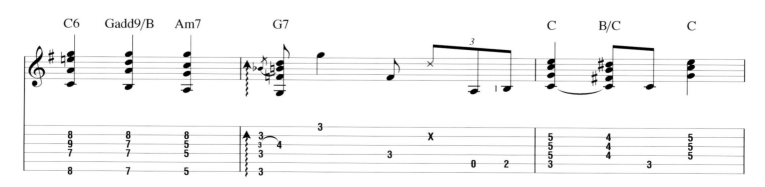

We Wish You a Merry Christmas

Traditional English Folksong

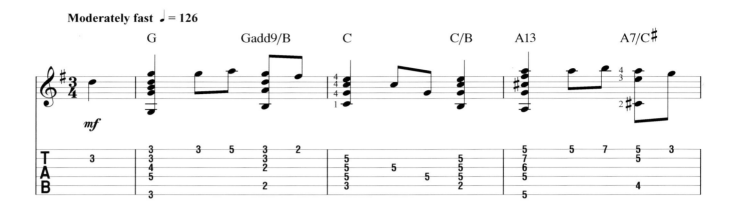

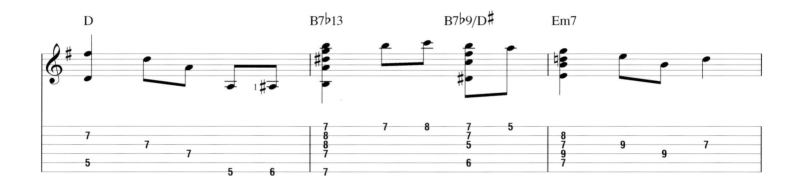

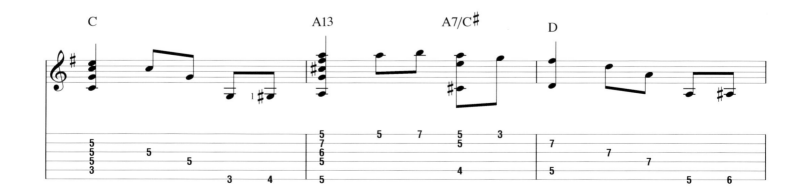

What Child Is This?

Words by William C. Dix
16th Century English Melody

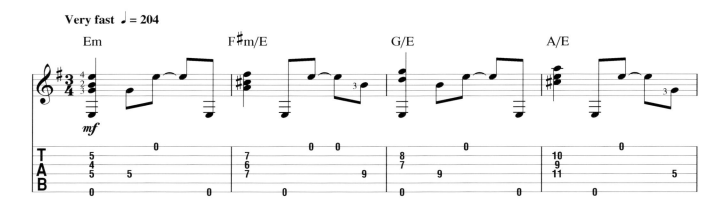

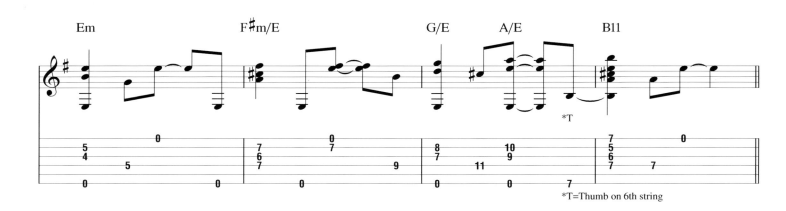

*T=Thumb on 6th string

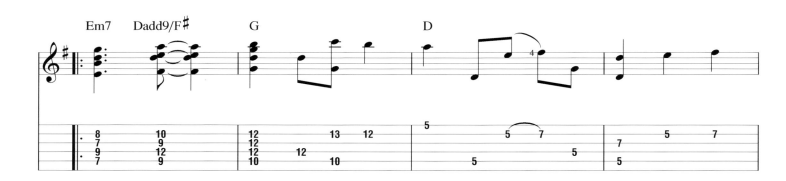

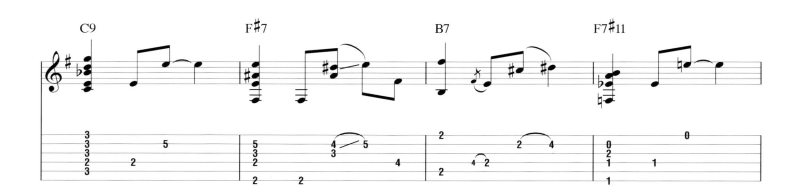

BIOGRAPHY

 JAKE REICHBART won WEMU-FM's Emily Remler scholarship for best jazz guitarist in 1991. Since then, he has been among the busiest freelance guitarists in the greater Detroit region. As a sideman, he appears on countless recordings and jingles and has performed alongside Motown legends and jazz greats alike, logging over 4,600 live gigs. His rock, funk, and blues chops can be heard on the accompanying CDs to several Hal Leonard instructional bass books by Jon Liebman.

Reichbart's passion, though, has always been solo guitar, citing Joe Pass and Tuck Andress as his main influences, while creating a unique voice of his own. He can arrange for the guitar nearly any tune imaginable, drawing from any and every musical style. His CDs *16 Songs* and *Long Ago and Far Away* have received nominations for best jazz recording at the Detroit Music Awards and have garnered rave reviews from such prestigious publications as *All Music Guide*, *Just Jazz Guitar*, and *Cadence*, as well as from numerous radio stations across the U.S. and abroad. He was featured on the front cover of the May 2012 issue of *Just Jazz Guitar* magazine, which included a lengthy interview and a transcription of one of his arrangements.

Jake cites his most enjoyable solo work as being the "restaurant guitarist," creating long-term relationships and enjoying a loyal following. For the past 22 years, he has been performing on Wednesday and Thursday evenings at Ann Arbor's most famous restaurant, The Earle.

IMPROVE YOUR IMPROV

AND OTHER JAZZ TECHNIQUES WITH BOOKS FROM HAL LEONARD

JAZZ GUITAR
HAL LEONARD GUITAR METHOD
by Jeff Schroedl
INCLUDES TAB

The Hal Leonard Jazz Guitar Method is your complete guide to learning jazz guitar. This book uses real jazz songs to teach the basics of accompanying and improvising jazz guitar in the style of Wes Montgomery, Joe Pass, Tal Farlow, Charlie Christian, Pat Martino, Barney Kessel, Jim Hall, and many others.
00695359 Book/Online Audio $19.99

AMAZING PHRASING
50 WAYS TO IMPROVE YOUR
IMPROVISATIONAL SKILLS • *by Tom Kolb*
INCLUDES TAB

This book explores all the main components necessary for crafting well-balanced rhythmic and melodic phrases. It also explains how these phrases are put together to form cohesive solos. Many styles are covered – rock, blues, jazz, fusion, country, Latin, funk and more – and all of the concepts are backed up with musical examples.
00695583 Book/Online Audio $19.99

BEST OF JAZZ GUITAR
by Wolf Marshall • Signature Licks
INCLUDES TAB

In this book/CD pack, Wolf Marshall provides a hands-on analysis of 10 of the most frequently played tunes in the jazz genre, as played by the leading guitarists of all time. Each selection includes technical analysis and performance notes, biographical sketches, and authentic matching audio with backing tracks.
00695586 Book/CD Pack.. $24.95

CHORD-MELODY PHRASES FOR GUITAR
by Ron Eschete • REH ProLessons Series
INCLUDES TAB

Expand your chord-melody chops with these outstanding jazz phrases! This book covers: chord substitutions, chromatic movements, contrary motion, pedal tones, inner-voice movements, reharmonization techniques, and much more. Includes standard notation and tab, and a CD.
00695628 Book/CD Pack.. $17.99

CHORDS FOR JAZZ GUITAR
THE COMPLETE GUIDE TO COMPING,
CHORD MELODY AND CHORD SOLOING • *by Charlton Johnson*

This book/audio pack will teach you how to play jazz chords all over the fretboard in a variety of styles and progressions. It covers: voicings, progressions, jazz chord theory, comping, chord melody, chord soloing, voice leading and many more topics. The audio offers 98 full-band demo tracks. No tablature.
00695706 Book/Online Audio $19.95

FRETBOARD ROADMAPS – JAZZ GUITAR
THE ESSENTIAL GUITAR PATTERNS
THAT ALL THE PROS KNOW AND USE • *by Fred Sokolow*

This book will get guitarists playing lead & rhythm anywhere on the fretboard, in any key! It teaches a variety of lead guitar styles using moveable patterns, double-note licks, sliding pentatonics and more, through easy-to-follow diagrams and instructions. The online audio includes 54 full-demo tracks.
00695354 Book/Online Audio $15.99

JAZZ IMPROVISATION FOR GUITAR
by Les Wise • REH ProLessons Series
INCLUDES TAB

This book/audio will allow you to make the transition from playing disjointed scales and arpeggios to playing melodic jazz solos that maintain continuity and interest for the listener. Topics covered include: tension and resolution, major scale, melodic minor scale, and harmonic minor scale patterns, common licks and substitution techniques, creating altered tension, and more! Features standard notation and tab, and online audio.
00695657 Book/Online Audio $17.99

JAZZ RHYTHM GUITAR
THE COMPLETE GUIDE
by Jack Grassel

This book/CD pack will help rhythm guitarists better understand: chord symbols and voicings, comping styles and patterns, equipment, accessories and set-up, the fingerboard, chord theory, and much more. The accompanying CD includes 74 full-band tracks.
00695654 Book/CD Pack.. $19.95

JAZZ SOLOS FOR GUITAR
LEAD GUITAR IN THE STYLES OF TAL FARLOW,
BARNEY KESSEL, WES MONTGOMERY, JOE PASS, JOHNNY SMITH
by Les Wise
INCLUDES TAB

Examine the solo concepts of the masters with this book including phrase-by-phrase performance notes, tips on arpeggio substitution, scale substitution, tension and resolution, jazz-blues, chord soloing, and more. The audio includes full demonstration and rhythm-only tracks.
00695447 Book/Online Audio $19.99

100 JAZZ LESSONS
Guitar Lesson Goldmine Series
by John Heussenstamm and Paul Silbergleit
INCLUDES TAB

Featuring 100 individual modules covering a giant array of topics, each lesson includes detailed instruction with playing examples presented in standard notation and tablature. You'll also get extremely useful tips, scale diagrams, and more to reinforce your learning experience, plus audio featuring performance demos of all the examples in the book!
00696454 Book/Online Audio $24.99

101 MUST-KNOW JAZZ LICKS
A QUICK, EASY REFERENCE GUIDE
FOR ALL GUITARISTS • *by Wolf Marshall*
INCLUDES TAB

Here are 101 definitive licks, plus demonstration audio, from every major jazz guitar style, neatly organized into easy-to-use categories. They're all here: swing and pre-bop, bebop, post-bop modern jazz, hard bop and cool jazz, modal jazz, soul jazz and postmodern jazz. Includes an introduction, tips, and a list of suggested recordings.
00695433 Book/Online Audio $17.99

SWING AND BIG BAND GUITAR
FOUR-TO-THE-BAR COMPING IN THE STYLE OF
FREDDIE GREEN • *by Charlton Johnson*

This unique package teaches the essentials of swing and big band styles, including chord voicings, inversions, substitutions; time and groove, reading charts, chord reduction, and expansion; sample songs, patterns, progressions, and exercises; chord reference library; and online audio with over 50 full-demo examples. Uses chord grids – no tablature.
00695147 Book/Online Audio $19.99

HAL•LEONARD®

Visit Hal Leonard Online at **www.halleonard.com**

*Prices, contents and availability
subject to change without notice.*

0918
126